Georgenes Medeiros

Ethical Hacking
For Beginners

By CC Palmer

Edition
English

"Ethical Hacking - For Beginners - 1st Edition
by CC Palmer - Translation: Georgenes Medeiros"

Index:

About the Editor

Georgenes Medeiros is Brazilian, graduated in Business Administration from Estácio de Sá College. He started in the field of research for editing and publishing digital content in 2018. The book was based on the work of CC Palmer, who wrote this piece in 2001.

The editor uses artificial intelligence for studying, editing, and translating digital content for various platforms and social networks. With no intention of plagiarism or copying original content. For anyone interested, I am available for assistance and freelance work on works. As for the copyright of the edition, it is registered with competent authorities in the region where it originated.

Introduction:

The explosive growth of the Internet has brought many good things: e-commerce, easy access to vast repositories of reference material, collaborative computing, email, and new avenues for advertising and information distribution, to name a few. Like most technological advances, there is also a dark side: criminal hackers.

Governments, businesses, and private citizens around the world are eager to be part of this revolution but fear that a hacker might invade their web server, replace their logo with pornography, read their emails, steal credit card numbers from an online shopping site, or implant software that secretly transmits their organization's secrets to the open Internet. With these concerns and more, the ethical hacker can help. This article describes ethical hackers: their skills, their attitudes, and how they assist their clients in finding and closing security gaps. The process of ethical hacking is explained, along with many of the issues that the Global Security Analysis Lab encountered during its early years of ethical hacking for IBM clients.

The process of ethical hacking involves a careful and systematic approach to identifying and fixing security vulnerabilities. Ethical hackers, also known as "white hats," use their skills to strengthen cybersecurity, acting in accordance with the law and adhering to strict ethical standards.

These professionals are experts in identifying potential weaknesses in systems, networks, and applications. By conducting penetration tests, they simulate real attacks to assess the resilience of the digital environment. Instead of exploiting these vulnerabilities to harm, ethical hackers document their findings and provide guidance on how to fix security flaws.

The Global Security Analysis Lab faced several challenges during its initial years in the field of ethical hacking for IBM clients. These challenges included the constant evolution of cyber threats, the need to stay updated on the latest hacking technologies and techniques, and collaboration with companies and organizations to create more secure digital environments.

As the digital society continues to grow, the demand for ethical hackers increases. Businesses and government entities recognize the importance of protecting their sensitive information and ensuring the integrity of their online operations. In this context, ethical hackers play a vital role, contributing to the construction of a safer and more reliable cyberspace.

Ethical hackers not only perform security assessments but also play a crucial role in raising awareness and training personnel.

They assist in creating robust security policies and implementing practices aimed at preventing cyber attacks. Additionally, they collaborate with incident response teams to develop efficient mitigation strategies in case of security breaches.

However, ethics in hacking go beyond technical skills. Ethical hackers must operate within legal and ethical boundaries, ensuring that their activities do not infringe on privacy or cause irreparable harm. Respect for the rights and integrity of organizations is fundamental to maintaining trust and legitimacy in the role of the ethical hacker in society.

The role of the Global Security Analysis Lab as a pioneer in the field of ethical hacking underscores the importance of facing the constant challenges in the evolving threat landscape. Continuous collaboration with IBM clients and adaptation to new technologies are crucial to maintaining effectiveness in identifying and resolving vulnerabilities.

As technology advances, the presence of ethical hackers becomes indispensable in protecting digital infrastructure. These professionals not only safeguard their clients' data and systems but also contribute to a more secure and resilient digital environment.

Furthermore, the ongoing improvement of ethical hackers' skills is essential to keep pace with the evolving tactics of malicious hackers. Continuous education, relevant certifications, and participation in cybersecurity communities are fundamental practices to ensure these professionals stay ahead of emerging threats.

Transparency plays a crucial role in the work of ethical hackers. By reporting their findings clearly and comprehensibly, they empower organizations to understand and address identified vulnerabilities. Effective communication between ethical hackers and stakeholders is paramount in building trust and facilitating the implementation of security measures.

Engaging interested parties is crucial to ensuring a prompt and efficient response as new threats emerge. Additionally, ethical hackers play a vital role in promoting a cybersecurity culture. They work to raise awareness among organizations and individuals about best security practices, encouraging the implementation of proactive measures to prevent potential breaches.

Ultimately, the work of ethical hackers is a crucial component in building a more secure and trustworthy digital ecosystem. By tackling the complex challenges of cyberspace with integrity and ethics, these professionals play an essential role in safeguarding data and preserving trust in the ever-evolving digital age.

Moreover, it is fundamental to recognize that ethical hacking is not only reactive but also proactive. Ethical hackers don't wait for security breaches to occur; instead, they anticipate and identify potential vulnerabilities before they become targets for malicious attacks.

This preventive approach is essential for strengthening an organization's security posture and mitigating potential risks. Ethical hackers also play a crucial role in researching emerging threats. By constantly analyzing the cybersecurity landscape, they can identify new techniques and strategies used by malicious hackers. This threat intelligence is valuable for enhancing cybersecurity defenses and developing more effective strategies against future attacks.

The collaboration between ethical hackers and organizations is crucial for success in protecting against cyber threats. This partnership enables organizations to better understand their vulnerabilities, implement effective solutions, and stay ahead of potential security risks.

In summary, ethical hackers play a multifaceted role in defending cybersecurity, acting as technical experts, educators, researchers, and strategic partners. Their contribution is essential to ensuring a resilient, secure, and trustworthy digital environment for individuals and organizations worldwide.

Beyond the technical aspect, ethics in hacking also involves a continuous commitment to legality and compliance.

Ethical hackers must operate within the limits established by laws and regulations, ensuring that their activities contribute to security without infringing legal rights. This adherence to ethical standards is essential to maintain the integrity of the profession and ensure the trust of organizations and society as a whole.

Responsible information sharing is another critical dimension of ethical hacking. While discovering and addressing vulnerabilities, ethical hackers must ensure that sensitive or confidential information is not improperly disclosed. Confidentiality is a cornerstone of the relationship between the ethical hacker and the client organization, strengthening mutual trust.

Additionally, continuous training is an indispensable practice for ethical hackers. As technologies evolve, new threats emerge, and the strategies of malicious hackers become more sophisticated, it is crucial to stay updated. Participating in courses, conferences, and collaborating with the cybersecurity community are ways to enhance the skills and knowledge necessary to face the ever-changing challenges of cyberspace.

Therefore, the ethical and responsible actions of ethical hackers are an essential pillar in building robust cybersecurity. By balancing technical skills, legal compliance, confidentiality, and continuous learning, these professionals play a vital role in protecting digital systems and promoting a secure online environment for all.

The integration of ethical hackers into the software development process is a growing trend, known as "Security by Design." This means that, instead of treating security as a later concern, ethical hackers are increasingly involved from the early stages of development. This proactive approach aims to incorporate secure practices from the outset, thereby reducing potential vulnerabilities and strengthening the resilience of digital systems.

Furthermore, ethical hacking ethics are sustained by collaboration among cybersecurity professionals. The exchange of information about new threats, techniques, and solutions is essential to address an ever-evolving landscape. Online communities and forums provide spaces to share knowledge, discuss best practices, and promote a collective approach to strengthen global cybersecurity.Os hackers éticos desempenham, ainda, um papel vital na educação pública sobre segurança cibernética.

Awareness of digital threats and preventive measures is crucial to empower end-users to protect their personal and professional information. In this context, ethical hackers often participate in educational initiatives, workshops, and awareness campaigns.

In summary, ethical hacking ethics go beyond the technical field, extending to a holistic approach that incorporates legal, collaborative, and educational aspects. In doing so, ethical hackers contribute not only to the security of specific systems but also to the building of a safer and more resilient digital culture. This integrated approach is crucial for addressing the increasingly complex and dynamic challenges of cyberspace.

Additionally, ethics in hacking also encompasses the social responsibility of ethical hackers. They have a responsibility to consider the broader impact of their actions, seeking to contribute to an inclusive and equitable digital environment. By identifying and addressing vulnerabilities, ethical hackers have the opportunity to promote digital security for a wide range of users, ensuring that everyone can benefit fairly and securely from digital technologies.

Diversity and inclusion in the field of cybersecurity are also crucial aspects. Encouraging and supporting the participation of a variety of perspectives and backgrounds helps create more comprehensive and effective solutions.

Ethical hackers play a crucial role in promoting inclusive work environments and inspiring a diversified new generation of cybersecurity professionals.

Another relevant point is the ethics in vulnerability disclosure. Ethical hackers need to adopt responsible practices when reporting security flaws to the affected organizations. Communicating appropriately and providing sufficient time for vulnerability correction is essential to ensure that organizations can protect their systems effectively before critical information becomes public.

Thus, the ethical conduct of ethical hackers goes beyond the mere application of technical skills; it incorporates a broader perspective, considering social impact, inclusion, responsibility, and transparency. By adopting a holistic approach, these professionals contribute not only to digital security but also to the construction of a more ethical, fair, and resilient digital ecosystem.

The term "hacker" has a dual application in the computer industry today. Initially, the term was defined as:

HACKER noun 1. A person who enjoys learning the details of computer systems and how to extend their capabilities, as opposed to most computer users who prefer to learn only the minimum necessary. 2. One who programs enthusiastically or who enjoys programming rather than just theorizing about programming. 1

This commendable description was often extended to the verbal form "hacking," which was used to describe the rapid creation of a new program or making changes to existing software, often in a clever way.

As computers became increasingly available in universities, user communities expanded beyond engineering or computer science researchers to other individuals who saw the computer as a curiously flexible tool. Whether they programmed computers for gaming, drawing, or to assist them in the more mundane tasks of their daily work, once computers were available for use, there was never a shortage of people wanting to use them.

Due to the increasing popularity of computers and their still high cost, access to them was often restricted. When denied access to computers, some users challenged the established access controls. They would steal passwords or account numbers by looking over someone's shoulder, explore the system for vulnerabilities they could exploit to bypass rules, or even take control of the entire system. They did these things to run programs of their choice or simply to alter the limitations under which their programs were running.

Initially, these computer intrusions were relatively harmless, with the most significant damage being the theft of computer time. On other occasions, these recreational activities resulted in the creation or modification of programs.

However, as technologies advanced and system interconnectivity increased, some of these activities began to take on a more malicious nature.

Over time, the term "hacker" came to be associated not only with enthusiasts and avid programmers but also with those who sought to exploit systems for personal gain, invading others' privacy, or causing significant harm.

The motivations varied, ranging from the simple pursuit of challenges to more harmful objectives, such as spreading viruses or conducting cyber attacks. This duality in the definition of "hacker" still persists today, requiring a distinction between ethical hackers, who use their skills to strengthen digital security, and malicious hackers, who seek to exploit vulnerabilities for harmful purposes. The field of cybersecurity continues to evolve, with ethics and legality being crucial in guiding the use of these technical skills in the ever-changing digital world.

In this scenario, professionals known as "ethical hackers" or "white hats" have emerged, playing a crucial role in defense against cyber threats. Ethical hackers apply their skills to identify and fix vulnerabilities in systems, networks, and applications. Unlike malicious hackers, their goal is to strengthen digital security, working collaboratively with organizations to protect sensitive information and ensure system integrity.

The practice of ethical hacking includes penetration testing, attack simulations, and comprehensive security assessments. Ethical hackers not only detect flaws but also provide guidance to strengthen defenses and prevent future attacks.

This proactive approach is essential in a digital environment where threats are constantly evolving. Ethical hacking goes beyond technical skills; it involves a commitment to legality, transparency, and integrity. Ethical hackers operate within strict boundaries, ensuring that their activities align with ethical standards and do not infringe on the privacy or security of third parties.

In the current cybersecurity landscape, where attacks and breaches are increasingly sophisticated, the presence of ethical hackers is vital. They play a crucial role in building a more secure digital infrastructure, protecting sensitive data, and promoting a cybersecurity culture. The evolution of this practice reflects the need to balance technological innovation with ethical responsibility, ensuring a trustworthy digital environment for everyone.

However, these intrusions did not remain benign for long. Occasionally, less skilled or less careful intruders would accidentally crash a system or damage its files, and system administrators had to restart it or make repairs. On other occasions, when these intruders were again denied access after the discovery of their activities, they reacted with intentionally destructive actions.

When the number of these destructive computer intrusions became noticeable, either due to system visibility or the extent of the inflicted damage, it became "news," and the media picked up the story. Instead of using the more accurate term "computer criminal," the media began using the term "hacker" to describe individuals who infiltrate computers for fun, revenge, or profit. Since calling someone a "hacker" was originally intended as a compliment, computer security professionals prefer to use the terms "cracker" or "intruder" for those hackers who turn to the dark side of hacking. For greater clarity, we will use the explicit terms "ethical hacker" and "criminal hacker" for the rest of this article.

What is ethical hacking?

With the growth of the Internet, computer security has become a significant concern for businesses and governments. They desire to leverage the Internet for e-commerce, advertising, distribution, and information access, among other activities, but they are concerned about the possibility of being "hacked." Simultaneously, potential clients of these services are concerned about maintaining control over personal information, ranging from credit card numbers to social security numbers and home addresses.

In the quest for an approach to deal with the problem, organizations have realized that one of the best ways to assess the threat of intruders to their interests is to have independent computer security professionals attempt to infiltrate their computer systems. This approach is similar to having independent auditors enter an organization to verify its accounting records. In the case of computer security, these "security teams" or "ethical hackers" would use the same tools and techniques as intruders, but they would not damage the target systems or steal information. Instead, they would assess the security of the target systems and report vulnerabilities found to the owners, along with instructions on how to address them.

Ethical hacking, therefore, involves a proactive approach to identify and rectify potential vulnerabilities in computer systems. Ethical hacking professionals, also known as "ethical hackers," work independently to simulate possible attacks, using the same techniques that a malicious intruder might employ. The crucial distinction is that they carry out these activities with the authorization and knowledge of the system owners.

These ethical hackers do not aim to cause harm or steal information; instead, their objective is to assist organizations in strengthening their defenses against cyber threats. Following their assessments, they provide detailed reports on the discovered vulnerabilities, offering guidance on how to remedy these security issues. This approach is crucial to ensure that organizations can take corrective measures before a real intruder can exploit these vulnerabilities.

The role of the ethical hacker is essential in building a robust security posture. With the constant evolution of cyber attack tactics, relying on dedicated professionals to explore and rectify vulnerabilities is a vital strategy for protecting an organization's critical data and systems. Thus, ethical hacking plays a significant role in defense against digital threats and in promoting a culture of cybersecurity.

This method of assessing the security of a system has been employed since the early days of computers. In one of the earliest ethical hacks, the United States Air Force conducted a "security assessment" on Multics operating systems for "potential use as a two-level (secret/top-secret) system."

Their assessment found that, although Multics was "significantly better than other conventional systems," it also had "vulnerabilities in hardware security, software security, and procedural security" that could be discovered with "relatively low effort." The authors conducted their tests following a realistic guide so that their results accurately represented the types of access an intruder could potentially achieve. They performed simple information-gathering tests as well as other tests that were direct attacks on the system, compromising its integrity. Clearly, their audience wanted to know both results. There are several other now-declassified reports describing ethical hacking activities within the U.S. military.

With the growth of computer networks and, especially, the Internet, studies on computer and network vulnerabilities began to appear outside the military environment. The work of Farmer and Venema, notable among these studies, was originally posted on Usenet in December 1993.

They publicly discussed, perhaps for the first time, the idea of using hacker techniques to assess the security of a system. With the goal of raising the overall level of security on the Internet and intranets, they described how they managed to gather enough information about their targets to compromise security if they chose to do so.

They provided several specific examples of how this information could be collected and exploited to gain control over the target, as well as how such attacks could be prevented. Farmer and Venema chose to freely share their report on the Internet so that everyone could read and learn from it. However, they realized that the tests in which they became so proficient could be too complex, time-consuming, or simply tedious for the typical system administrator to perform regularly. For this reason, they gathered all the tools they had used during their work, packaged them into a single, easy-to-use application, and made it available for free to anyone who chose to download it. Their program, called Security Analysis Tool for Auditing Networks, or SATAN, received significant media attention worldwide. Most of this initial attention was negative because the program's capabilities were perceived as security threats, despite its intention to strengthen cyber defenses. However, Farmer and Venema argued that understanding vulnerabilities was crucial to adequately protect systems against real attacks.

The capabilities of SATAN were misunderstood. The tool was not an automated hacking program that would invade systems and steal their secrets.

On the contrary, the tool performed an audit that identified a system's vulnerabilities and provided advice on how to eliminate them. Just as banks undergo regular audits of their accounts and procedures, computer systems also need regular checks. SATAN provided this auditing capability but went a step further by also advising the user on how to address the issues it discovered. The tool did not inform the user how the vulnerability could be exploited because there would be no practical utility in doing so.

Despite Farmer and Venema's intentions to strengthen cyber defenses, the initial attention to SATAN was predominantly negative, with concerns about its ability to expose potential vulnerabilities. However, it is crucial to clarify that SATAN was not an invasion tool but rather an assessment and security improvement tool.

SATAN addressed the crucial need for regularly assessing the security of systems, akin to regular financial audits in banking institutions. Instead of just identifying vulnerabilities, the tool also provided constructive guidance on how to fix the detected issues. This approach not only highlighted weaknesses but also offered solutions to strengthen security.

Farmer and Venema's decision to share SATAN for free reflects their commitment to raising the overall level of security on the Internet. The idea was to empower system administrators, even those with limited resources, to perform regular checks on their systems and address potential vulnerabilities. This contributed to a more conscious and proactive culture regarding cybersecurity.

The initial controversy surrounding SATAN highlights the challenges associated with introducing ethical hacking tools. However, time has shown that Farmer and Venema's approach was visionary, emphasizing the importance of understanding and correcting vulnerabilities to ensure safer digital environments. SATAN played a pioneering role in paving the way for cybersecurity awareness and encouraged the adoption of ethical hacking practices in an effort to protect system integrity.

Who are ethical hackers?

These early efforts provide good examples of ethical hackers. Successful ethical hackers possess a variety of skills. Firstly, they must be entirely trustworthy. While testing a client's system security, the ethical hacker may come across information about the client that should remain confidential. In many cases, disclosing such information could lead real attackers to compromise the systems, potentially resulting in financial losses. During an assessment, the ethical hacker often holds the "keys to the kingdom" and, therefore, must be trustworthy to exercise strict control over any information about a target that could be misused. The sensitivity of the information collected during an assessment requires stringent measures to ensure the security of systems used by ethical hackers: limited-access labs with physical security protection and floor-to-ceiling walls, multiple secure Internet connections, a safe for storing clients' paper documentation, robust encryption to protect electronic results, and isolated networks for testing.

Ethical hackers typically have very strong skills in programming and computer networks and significant expertise in the field of computing and networking.

They are also proficient in installing and maintaining systems using the most popular operating systems (e.g., UNIX** or Windows NT**) used on target systems. These basic skills are complemented with detailed knowledge of the hardware and software provided by the most popular computer and network hardware manufacturers. It's worth noting that additional specialization in security is not always necessary, as strong skills in other areas imply a very good understanding of how security is maintained across various systems. These system management skills are necessary for the actual testing of vulnerabilities but are equally important when preparing the report for the client after the test.

Finally, good candidates for ethical hacking have more determination and patience than most people. Unlike the way someone breaks into a computer in movies, the work that ethical hackers perform requires a lot of time and persistence. This is a critical characteristic, as criminal hackers are known to be extremely patient and willing to monitor systems for days or weeks while waiting for an opportunity. A typical assessment may require several days of tedious work that is difficult to automate. Some parts of assessments must be done outside normal working hours to avoid disruptions to production on "live" targets or to simulate the timing of a real attack.

When encountering a system they are not familiar with, ethical hackers dedicate time to learn about the system and attempt to identify its vulnerabilities. Lastly, staying updated with the ever-changing world of computer and network security requires continuous education and review.

It can be observed that the skills we've described could belong to both a criminal hacker and an ethical hacker. Just as in sports or war, knowledge of your opponent's skills and techniques is vital for your success. In the realm of computer security, the task of the ethical hacker is the most challenging. In traditional crime, anyone can become a burglar, a graffiti artist, or a robber. Their potential targets are often easy to identify and tend to be localized. Local law enforcement needs to know how criminals ply their trade and how to stop them. On the internet, anyone can download tools used by criminal hackers and use them to attempt to infiltrate computers anywhere in the world. Ethical hackers need to know the techniques of criminal hackers, how their activities can be detected, and how to stop them.

Furthermore, it is important to emphasize that, unlike criminal hackers, ethical hackers do not seek to exploit vulnerabilities for malicious purposes.

Instead, their goal is to enhance digital security by identifying and rectifying potential flaws before they can be exploited by malicious individuals.

In the ethical hacking scenario, ethics play a crucial role. Trust between the ethical hacker and the client is fundamental, as the hacker has access to sensitive information during the assessment. Integrity and ethical responsibility are essential values that ethical hackers must uphold, ensuring that the disclosure of vulnerabilities is done responsibly and that any confidential information is handled with due care.

In addition to technical skills and ethics, ethical hackers also need a considerable amount of determination and patience. Ethical hacking work involves conducting detailed and thorough assessments, often requiring extended periods of analysis. Persistence is crucial, especially when dealing with unfamiliar systems, where time needs to be dedicated to understanding the infrastructure and uncovering potential weaknesses.

Finally, it's important to recognize that ethical hacking is a dynamic discipline that requires constant updating. With the rapid evolution of security technologies and new cyber threats emerging regularly, ethical hackers need to stay informed about the latest trends and techniques in the field of digital security.

Continuous learning is essential to ensure they are always ahead of emerging challenges and can provide the best security solutions for their clients.

Given these qualifications, how do you find such individuals? The best candidates for ethical hackers often have successfully published research or have released popular open-source security software. The computer security community is strongly self-regulated, given the importance of their work. Most ethical hackers, and many of the best computer and network security experts, didn't start by focusing on these issues. Many of them were computer users from various disciplines, such as astronomy and physics, mathematics, computer science, philosophy, or liberal arts, who took it personally when someone interrupted their work with a hack.

One rule that the IBM ethical hacking effort had from the beginning was that we didn't hire ex-hackers. Although some argue that only a "true hacker" would have the skill to actually do the job, we felt that the requirement for absolute trust eliminated such candidates.

We compared the decision to hiring a fire chief for a school district: even though a former talented arsonist may really know everything about starting and extinguishing fires, would parents of students feel comfortable with such a choice? This decision was further justified when the service was initially offered: the clients themselves requested that such a restriction be observed.

Since the formation of the IBM ethical hacking group, there have been numerous former hackers who became security consultants and spokespersons for the media. Although they may have moved away from the "dark side," doubts will always linger.

What do ethical hackers do?

The assessment by an ethical hacker of a system's security seeks answers to three basic questions:

- What can an intruder see in the target systems?

- What can an intruder do with this information?

- Does anyone on the target notice the intruder's attempts or successes?

While the first and second of these points are clearly important, the third is even more crucial: if the owners or operators of the target systems do not perceive when someone is trying to invade, intruders can and will spend weeks or months attempting, usually ending up successful.

When a client requests an assessment, there is much discussion and paperwork that must be done in advance. The discussion begins with the client's answers to questions similar to those posed by Garfinkel and Spafford:

1. What are you trying to protect?

2. What are you trying to protect against?

3. How much time, effort, and money are you willing to spend to obtain adequate protection?

A surprising number of clients have difficulty answering the first question precisely: a medical center may say "our patient information," an engineering company may answer "our new product designs," and an online retailer may respond "our customer database."

All of these answers are insufficient as they describe the targets in a general manner. Often, the client needs to be guided to succinctly describe all critical information assets for which the loss could adversely affect the organization or its customers. These assets should also include sources of secondary information, such as employee names and addresses (which are privacy and security risks), computer and network information (which could aid an intruder), and other organizations with which that organization collaborates (providing alternative paths to the target systems through a possibly less secure partner).

A complete answer to (2) specifies more than just the loss of things listed in the answer to (1). There are also issues of system availability, where a denial-of-service attack could cost the client actual revenue and loss of customers because the systems were unavailable.

The world became quite familiar with denial-of-service attacks in February 2000 when attacks were launched against eBay, Yahoo!, E*TRADE, CNN, and other popular sites. During the attacks, customers were unable to access these sites, resulting in revenue loss and "market share." The answers to (1) should contain more than just a list of information assets in the organization's computing.

The level of damage to an organization's good image resulting from a successful criminal hack can range from merely embarrassing to a serious threat to revenue. As an example of a hack affecting an organization's image, on January 17, 2000, a website of the U.S. Library of Congress was attacked. The original home screen is shown in Figure 1, while the hacked screen is shown in Figure 2. As is often done, the criminal hacker left his nickname, or handle, near the top of the page to ensure credit for the intrusion.

Figure 1 Library of Congress webpage before the attack

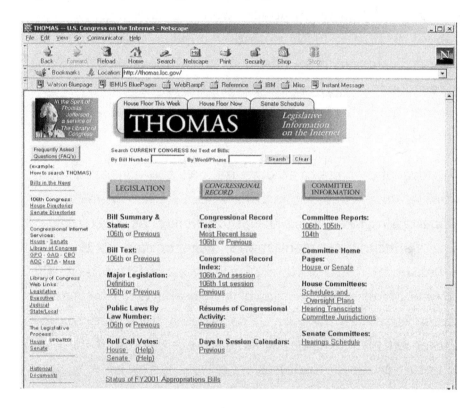

Clients often have the mistaken impression that their website would not be a target. They cite numerous reasons, such as "there's nothing interesting on it" or "hackers have never heard of my company." What these clients fail to realize is that every website is a target. The goal of many criminal hackers is simple: to do something spectacular and make sure all their friends know they did it.

Another rebuttal is that many hackers simply don't care about who your company or organization is; they hack your site because they can. For example, web administrators at UNICEF (United Nations Children's Fund) might well have thought that no hacker would target them. However, in January 1998, their page was defaced, as shown in Figures 3 and 4. Many other examples of hacked web pages can be found on web archive sites.

The answers to the third question are complicated by the fact that the costs of computer and network security come in three forms. First, there are the actual monetary costs incurred when obtaining security consulting, hiring personnel, and deploying hardware and software to meet security needs. Second, there is the cost of usability: the more secure a system is, the harder it may be to make it easy to use.

Difficulty can manifest in the form of obscure password selection rules, strict system configuration rules, and limited remote access. Third, there is the cost of computer and network performance. The more time a computer or network spends on security needs, such as strong encryption and detailed system activity logging, the less time it has to deal with user issues.

Due to Moore's Law, this may be less concerning for mainframes, desktops, and laptops. However, it still remains a concern for mobile computing.

Figure 2 Hacked Library of Congress Web Page

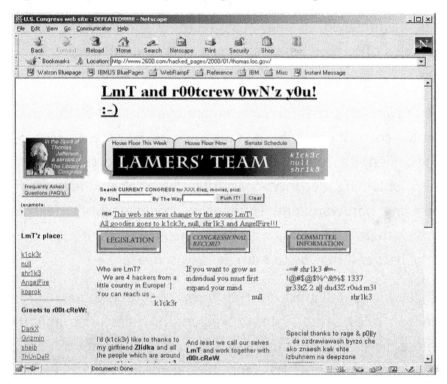

Get out of prison"

Once the answers to these three questions have been determined, a security assessment plan is drafted, identifying the systems to be tested, how they should be tested, and any limitations on that testing.

Commonly known as the "get out of jail free" card, this contractual agreement between the client and ethical hackers, typically crafted collaboratively by both parties, is the "get out of jail free" card. This agreement also protects ethical hackers from legal action since much of what they do during an assessment would be illegal in most countries. The agreement provides an accurate description, often in the form of network addresses or modem phone numbers, of the systems to be assessed. Accuracy at this point is of utmost importance as a small mistake could lead to assessing the wrong system at the client's facilities or, in the worst case, assessing the system of some other organization.

Figure 3 UNICEF web page before the attack

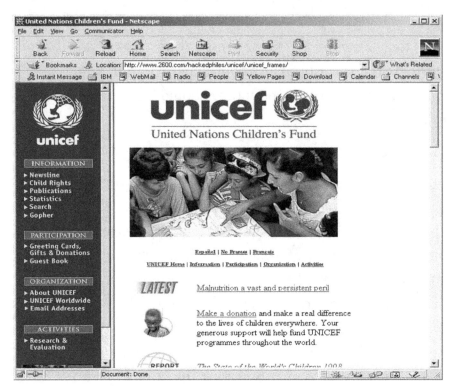

Once the target systems are identified, the agreement should describe how they are to be tested. The best assessment is done under an "unrestricted" approach. This means that the ethical hacker can try anything they can think of to attempt to gain access or disrupt the target system. While this is the most realistic and useful, some clients hesitate at this level of testing.

Clients have various reasons for this, the most common of which is that the target systems are "in production," and interfering with their operation could be detrimental to the organization's interests. However, it should be pointed out to these clients that these very reasons are precisely why an "unrestricted" approach should be employed. An intruder will not be playing by the client's rules. If the systems are so crucial to the organization's well-being, they should be tested as comprehensively as possible. In either case, the client should be fully aware of the inherent risks in ethical hacking assessments. These risks include alerting the staff and unintentional system failures, degradation of network or system performance, denial of service, and log file size explosions.

Figure 4 UNICEF Webpage Hacked

Some clients insist that once ethical hackers gain access to their network or one of their systems, the assessment should be halted, and the client notified.

This kind of decision should be discouraged as it prevents the client from learning everything ethical hackers can discover about their systems. It may also lead the client to have a false sense of security, thinking that the first security issue found is the only one present. The assessment should be allowed to continue because where there is one exposure, there likely are others.

The schedule of assessments can also be important for the client. The client may wish to avoid affecting systems and networks during regular working hours. Although this restriction is not recommended, it only slightly reduces the accuracy of the assessment since most attackers perform their work outside regular local working hours. However, attacks made during regular working hours may be more easily concealed. Intrusion detection system alerts may even be disabled or less carefully monitored during the day. Regardless of the agreed-upon schedule, the client should provide contacts within the organization who can respond to ethical hackers' calls if a system or network appears to have been adversely affected by the assessment or if an extremely dangerous vulnerability is found and needs to be immediately addressed.

It is common for potential clients to postpone the assessment of their systems until a few weeks or days before they need to go into operation. Such last-minute assessments have little value as implementing fixes for discovered security issues may take longer than is available and may introduce new problems into the system.

For the client to receive a valid assessment, they should be alerted to limit prior knowledge of the test as much as possible. Otherwise, ethical hackers may find the electronic equivalent of the client's employees running ahead of them, locking doors and windows. By limiting the number of people in the target organization who know about the impending assessment, the likelihood increases that the assessment reflects the actual security posture of the organization. A related issue the client should be prepared to address is the relationship of ethical hackers with the employees of the target organization. Employees may see this "surprise inspection" as a threat to their jobs, so the management team of the organization must be prepared to take steps to reassure them.

The ethical hack itself

Once the contractual agreement is in effect, the tests can commence as defined in the agreement. It should be noted that the tests themselves pose some risk to the client, as a criminal hacker monitoring the transmissions of ethical hackers could obtain the same information. If ethical hackers identify a security weakness in the client, a criminal hacker could potentially attempt to exploit that vulnerability. This is particularly concerning because the activities of ethical hackers may mask those of criminal hackers. The best approach to this dilemma is to maintain multiple addresses across the internet from which the transmissions of ethical hackers will originate and to switch source addresses frequently. Comprehensive records of the tests conducted by ethical hackers are always kept, both for the final report and in case anything unusual occurs. In extreme cases, additional intrusion monitoring software may be deployed on the target to ensure that all tests come from the machines of ethical hackers. However, this is difficult to do without alerting the client's staff and may require the cooperation of the client's internet service provider.

The line between criminal hacking and the writing of computer viruses is becoming increasingly blurred.

When requested by the client, the ethical hacker can conduct tests to determine the client's vulnerability to email or web-based virus vectors. However, it is much better for the client to deploy strong antivirus software, keep it updated, and have a clear and simple policy for incident reporting. IBM's Cyber Security Immune System is another approach that provides additional capability to recognize new viruses and report them to a central laboratory that automatically analyzes the virus and provides an immediate vaccine.

As depicted in Figure 5, there are various types of tests. Any combination of the following can be requested:

- **Remote Network:** This test simulates an intruder launching an attack over the internet. The primary defenses to be defeated here are border firewalls, filtering routers, and web servers.

- **Remote Dial-up Network:** This test simulates an intruder launching an attack against the client's modem pools. The main defenses to be defeated here are user authentication schemes. These types of tests should be coordinated with the local telephone company.

Figure 5 Different ways to attack computer security

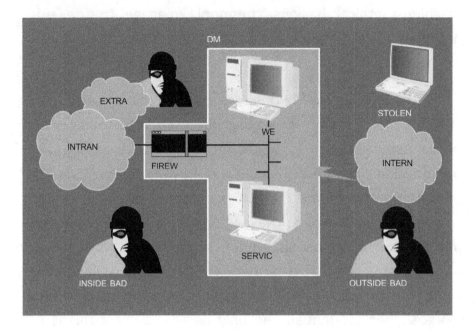

- **Local Network:** This test simulates an employee or another authorized person who has a legal connection to the organization's network. The main defenses to be defeated here are intranet firewalls, internal web servers, server security measures, and email systems.

- **Stolen Notebook:** In this test, the notebook of a key employee, such as a senior manager or strategist, is handed over to ethical hackers without prior notice. They examine the computer for stored passwords in dialing software, corporate information assets, personal information, etc.

Since many busy users store their passwords on their machines, ethical hackers commonly manage to use this notebook to dial into the corporate intranet with the owner's full privileges.

- **Social Engineering:** This test assesses the organization's staff for the possibility of leaking information to someone. A typical example of this would be an intruder calling the organization's computer helpdesk and asking for the external phone numbers of the modem pool. Defending against this type of attack is the most challenging as it involves people and personalities. Most people are inherently helpful, so it seems harmless to tell someone who appears lost where the computer room is, or to allow someone into the building who "forgot" their credential. The only defense against this is to increase security awareness.

- **Physical Entry:** This test simulates a physical penetration of the organization's building. Special arrangements must be made for this, as security guards or the police may get involved if ethical hackers fail to avoid detection. Once inside the building, it is crucial that the tester is not detected. One technique is for the tester to carry a document with the logo of the target company. Such a document could be found by rummaging through trash before the ethical hack or casually picking up a document from a trash can or desk once the tester is inside.

The main defenses here include a robust security policy, guards, access controls and monitoring, and security awareness.

Each of these types of tests can be conducted from three perspectives: as a total stranger, a "semi-stranger," or a valid user.

- A total stranger has very limited knowledge about the target systems. The only information used is available through public sources on the Internet. This test represents the most commonly perceived threat. A well-defended system should not allow this type of intruder to do anything.

- A semi-stranger has limited access to one or more of the organization's computers or networks. This tests scenarios such as a bank allowing its depositors to use special software and a modem to access information about their accounts. A well-defended system should only allow this type of intruder to access information about their own account.

- A valid user has valid access to at least some of the organization's computers and networks. This tests whether insiders with some access can extend that access beyond what was prescribed. A well-defended system should allow an insider to access only the areas and resources assigned by the system administrator.

- The actual assessment of the client's systems progresses through various phases, as described earlier by Boulanger.

The Final Report

The final report is a compilation of all the findings made by the ethical hacker during the assessment. The discovered vulnerabilities are explained, and prevention procedures are specified. If the activities of the ethical hacker were noticed, the response of the client's team is described, and suggestions for improvements are offered. If social engineering tests exposed problems, advice is given on how to increase awareness. This is the main point of the entire exercise: it's not enough just to tell clients they have issues. The report should include specific advice on how to close the vulnerabilities and keep them closed. The actual techniques employed by the testers are never revealed. This is because the person delivering the report can never be sure who will have access to that report when it's in the client's hands. For example, an employee might want to try some of the techniques themselves. They might choose to test the company's systems, possibly annoying system administrators or even inadvertently concealing a real attack.

The employee may also choose to test the systems of another organization, which is a crime in the United States when done without permission. The actual delivery of the report is also a delicate matter. If vulnerabilities were found, the report can be extremely dangerous if it falls into the wrong hands.

A competitor could use it for corporate espionage, a hacker could use it to invade the client's computers, or a prankster could simply post the content of the report on the web as a joke. The final report is usually delivered directly to an executive of the client organization in printed format. Ethical hackers would have the ongoing responsibility of ensuring the security of any information they retain; thus, in most cases, all job-related information is destroyed at the end of the contract.

Once the ethical hack is completed and the report delivered, the client may ask, "So, if I fix these things, I'll have perfect security, right?" Unfortunately, that is not the case. People operate the client's computers and networks, and people make mistakes. The longer it has been since the test was conducted, the less reliably one can say about the state of the client's security. A part of the final report includes recommendations for the steps the client should continue to follow to mitigate the impact of these errors in the future.

Conclusions

The idea of testing the security of a system by attempting to invade it is not new. Whether it's a car manufacturer testing car collisions or an individual testing martial arts skills by sparring with a partner, evaluation through testing under the attack of a real adversary is widely accepted as prudent. However, this alone is not sufficient. As Roger Schell noted almost 30 years ago:

> "From a practical standpoint, the security problem will persist as long as manufacturers remain committed to current system architectures produced without a firm security requirement. As long as there is support for ad hoc fixes and security patches for these inadequate designs, and as long as the illusory results of penetration teams are accepted as demonstrations of computer system security, adequate security will not be a reality."

Regular auditing, vigilant intrusion detection, good system administration practices, and computer security awareness are essential components of an organization's security efforts. A single failure in any of these areas can expose an organization to cyber-vandalism, embarrassment, loss of revenue or market share, or worse.

Any new technology comes with its benefits and risks. While ethical hackers can assist clients in better understanding their security needs, it is up to the clients to keep their defenses in place.

Thanks

The author would like to thank several people: the members of the Global Security Analysis Laboratory at IBM Research for sharing their incredible expertise and ability to make virtually anyone understand more about security; Chip Coy and Nick Simicich for their pioneering work in defining IBM's Security Consulting Practice in the early days; and Paul Karger for his encyclopedic knowledge in computer security research and his amazing ability to produce copies of all notable articles on the subject that have been published.

References and Notes Cited:

Certainly! Here's a brief summary of the references you provided:

1. **"The New Hacker's Dictionary" by E. S. Raymond (1991, MIT Press, Cambridge, MA):** This book likely explores the terminology and jargon used in the hacker culture, providing insights into the language and expressions commonly used among hackers.

2. **"Database Nation" by S. Garfinkel (2000, O'Reilly & Associates, Cambridge, MA):** This book, authored by Simson Garfinkel, may delve into issues related to privacy and surveillance in the context of databases and information systems.

3. **The term "hackers éticos" (ethical hackers) was first used in an interview with John Patrick of IBM by Gary Athens, published in the June 1995 edition of ComputerWorld.**

4. **"Multics Security Evaluation: Vulnerability Analysis" by P. A. Karger and R. R. Schell (June 1974, ESD-TR-74-193, Hanscom Air Force Base, MA):** This technical report likely discusses the security evaluation and vulnerability analysis of the Multics operating system.

5. **"OS/360 Computer Security Penetration Exercise" by S. M. Goheen and R. S. Fiske (October 16, 1972, WP-4467, The MITRE Corporation, Bedford, MA):** This document may detail a penetration exercise conducted on the OS/360 computer security, likely providing insights into vulnerabilities and security measures.

6. **"Security Analysis and Enhancements of Computer Operating Systems" by R. P. Abbott, J. S. Chen, J. E. Donnelly, W. L. Konigsford, and S. T. Tokubo (April 1976, NBSIR 76-1041, National Bureau of Standards, Washington, DC):** This report might cover security analyses and improvements related to computer operating systems, particularly focusing on enhancing security measures.

7. W. M. Inglis, "Security Problems in the WWMCCS GCOS System," Joint Technical Support Activity Operating System Technical Bulletin 730S-12, Defense Communications Agency (2 August 1973).

8. D. Farmer and W. Z. Venema, "Improving the Security of Your Site by Breaking into It," originally published on Usenet (December 1993); It has since been updated and is available at ftp://ftp.porcupine.org/pub/security/index.html#documents.

9. See http://www.faqs.org/usenet/.

10. Who can really determine who said something first on the Internet?

11. See http://www.cs.ruu.nl/cert-uu/satan.html.

12. This strategy is based on the ideal of increasing the security of the entire Internet by providing security software for free. This way, no one will have excuses for not taking measures to improve security.

13. S. Garfinkel and E. Spafford, "Practical Unix Security," First Edition, O'Reilly & Associates, Cambridge, MA (1996).

14. For a collection of previously hacked Web sites, see http://www.2600.com/hacked_pages/ or http://defaced.alldes.de. However, be warned that some of the hacked pages may contain pornographic images.

15. In 1965, Intel co-founder Gordon Moore was preparing a speech and made a memorable remark. When he started graphing data on the growth in performance of memory chips, he noticed a striking trend. Each new chip contained approximately twice the capacity of its predecessor, and each chip was released approximately every 18 to 24 months of the previous chip. In subsequent years, the pace slowed somewhat, but data density doubled approximately every 18 months, and this is the current definition of Moore's Law.

16. J. O. Kephart, G. B. Sorkin, D. M. Chess e S. R. White, "Fighting Computer Viruses," Scientific American 277, Nº 5, 88–93 (novembro de 1997).

17. Veja http://www.research.ibm.com/antivirus/SciPapers.htm para papers adicionais de pesquisa antivírus.

18. A. Boulanger, "Catapults and Grappling Hooks: The Tools and Techniques of Information Warfare," IBM Systems Journal 37, Nº 1, 106–114 (1998).

19. R. R. Schell, P. J. Downey e G. J. Popek, "Preliminary Notes on the Design of Secure Military Computer Systems," MCI-73-1, ESD/AFSC, Hanscom Air Force Base, Bedford, MA (janeiro de 1973).

Accepted for publication on April 13, 2001.

*Charles C. Palmer IBM Research Division, Thomas J. Watson Research Center, P.O. Box 218, Yorktown Heights, New York 10598 (e-mail: ccpalmer@us.ibm.com). Dr. Palmer manages the Network Security and Cryptography department at the IBM Thomas J. Watson Research Center. His teams work in the research areas of cryptography, Internet security technologies, JavaTM security, privacy, and the Global Security Analysis Lab (GSAL), which he co-founded in 1995. As part of GSAL, Dr. Palmer has worked with IBM Global Services to launch IBM's ethical hacking practice. He frequently speaks on computer and network security topics at conferences around the world.

.

He was also an associate professor of computer science at Polytechnic University, Hawthorne, New York, from 1993 to 1997. He holds four patents and has published several publications on his work at IBM and the Polytechnic.*

Ethical Hacking for Beginners - 1 Edition

Editing, Translation and adaptation: Georgenes Medeiros

Writer: CC Palmer

Copyright © 2024

www.ingramcontent.com/pod-product-compliance
Lightning Source LLC
LaVergne TN
LVHW052056060326
832903LV00061B/1045